EDGE
BOOKS

The Unexplained

ESP:
Extrasensory Perception

by **Michael Martin**

Consultants:
Dean Radin, Senior Scientist, and
Marilyn Schlitz, Vice President for Research and Education
Institute of Noetic Sciences
Petaluma, California

Capstone
press

Mankato, Minnesota

Edge Books are published by Capstone Press,
151 Good Counsel Drive, P.O. Box 669, Mankato, Minnesota 56002.
www.capstonepress.com

Library of Congress Cataloging-in-Publication Data
Martin, Michael, 1948–
    ESP : extrasensory perception / by Michael Martin.
    p. cm.—(Edge books. The Unexplained)
    Includes bibliographical references and index.
    ISBN-13: 978-0-7368-5451-1 (hardcover)
    ISBN-10: 0-7368-5451-7 (hardcover)
    1. Extrasensory perception—Juvenile literature. I. Title. II. Series.
BF1321.M365 2006
133.8—dc22   2005018488

Summary: Describes the history, studies, and search for the causes of ESP.

Editorial Credits
Katy Kudela, editor; Juliette Peters, set designer; Kate Opseth and Thomas Emery,
    book designers; Kelly Garvin, photo researcher/photo editor

Photo Credits
Capstone Press/Karon Dubke, cover
Corbis/Jeffrey Allan Salter, 27; Mika, 5; NASA/Roger Ressmeyer, 25
Fortean Picture Library/Dr. Elmar R. Gruber, 29; Dr. Susan Blackmore, 21;
    Philip Panton, 8
Getty Images Inc./Hulton Archive, 7; James Oliver, 23; Jeff Spielman, 17
Mary Evans Picture Library, 11, 12, 14, 15; John Cutten, 18, 19

1 2 3 4 5 6 11 10 09 08 07 06

Table of Contents

FEATURES

Chapter 1

Mysteries of the Mind

One morning, a man kept $2 from a bank deposit to buy a lottery ticket. He rarely bought lottery tickets. But he had a strange feeling that his ticket would be a winner. This feeling was nothing new to the man. He had experienced such feelings since he was a child.

Before buying the ticket, the man went home to talk to his wife. He told her he would win $200 from an orange lottery ticket.

Later in the day, the man walked into a gas station. He saw a display for a new lottery game. The man walked up to the counter and discovered the tickets were orange. He bought one ticket. The ticket was a $200 winner.

Learn about:
- ESP versus luck
- A frightening dream
- Reading minds

Some people believe ESP lets them know what the future holds.

How did the man know he would buy a winning lottery ticket? Some people would say the man was just lucky. Everyone hopes they will be lucky when they play the lottery. But maybe this man had more than luck. He might have had an extrasensory perception (ESP) experience.

What is ESP?

Some people call ESP a sixth sense. Like sight, hearing, smell, taste, and touch, ESP helps people to understand the world they live in. Not everyone has ESP experiences. But people who do have them seem to gather information in unusual ways.

Precognition is one form of ESP. The man with the lottery ticket seemed to have this sense. He knew he would win the lottery before it happened.

Sometimes precognition shows up in dreams. In 1966, a schoolgirl in Wales had such an experience. Ten-year-old Eryl Mai Jones lived in a coal mining town. One night, she dreamed that something black completely covered her school. The next morning, she told her mother about the dream.

Two days later, at 9:15 in the morning, an avalanche of coal, sludge, water, and rocks covered parts of the town. Jones' school was destroyed. She and more than 100 of her classmates were killed.

Other Forms of ESP

Some forms of ESP are thought to help people communicate. People with telepathy can share thoughts with each other without speaking. They can read thoughts even when the other person is far away.

▼ People who use telepathy claim to sense the thoughts of others.

Parents sometimes tell stories of their children reading minds. During supper one evening, a woman in Pennsylvania was going to ask her husband to call a workman. Before she could speak, the woman's 3-year-old daughter blurted out the workman's name.

Another kind of ESP is called clairvoyance. People who are clairvoyant sense people and events from a distance. The police have used clairvoyants to help them find missing people, murder victims, and crime suspects. The U.S. military has also used clairvoyants to find missing planes and ships.

Fact or Fiction?

Millions of people around the world believe they have had ESP experiences. But many other people still don't believe in ESP. Some scientists say that ESP can't be real because it doesn't obey the laws of nature. They also think ESP evidence is weak.

Yet these doubts haven't stopped ESP researchers. They know how difficult it is to prove ESP is real. They want a better understanding of the powers of the human mind.

Chapter 2

History of ESP

For thousands of years, people have told stories of ESP experiences. But it was not until the 1880s that scientists began to study ESP.

In 1882, the Society for Psychical Research formed in England. Its members wanted to find out whether life existed after death. They studied ghosts and haunted houses. They also gathered information about ESP experiences. They found that many people have unexplained experiences.

Learn about:
- A famous vision
- An author's experiments
- Dr. J. B. Rhine

In the 1800s, people began testing
to find out if they could read
someone else's thoughts.

A Vision of Fire

People around the world have reported ESP experiences. One famous clairvoyant experience happened to a scientist in Sweden.

In 1759, Emmanuel Swedenborg was at a dinner party 300 miles (483 kilometers) away from his home. He had a sudden, terrifying vision. Swedenborg told other guests that a fire was raging near his home.

Swedenborg described many details of the fire. He said the fire stopped three houses from his own at 8:00 that night. A messenger later said that Swedenborg's descriptions of the fire were true.

Emmanuel Swedenborg

EDGE FACT

Early ESP Experiments

In 1930, Upton Sinclair wrote *Mental Radio*. This book told of Sinclair's telepathic studies with his wife, Mary. It increased people's interest in ESP.

During one of Sinclair's experiments, a person in one room drew a picture. Mary sat in another room. She then copied the other person's drawing without ever seeing it. Mary's ability was not limited by distance. She could copy a drawing even when the other person was far away.

Many people doubted Sinclair's experiments. They thought he and his wife were trying to trick people into buying more of his books. Researchers began to look for stronger proof that ESP was real.

During the 1930s, a scientist at North Carolina's Duke University began to test ESP abilities. Dr. J. B. Rhine used Zener cards. Each card had a symbol on one side.

Rhine asked volunteers to guess the symbol on each card. People were expected to guess one of every five cards correctly by chance. But some people guessed much better than others.

Rhine's experiments suggested that some people sense things in unknown ways. His studies showed that ESP could be tested with science. Even more scientists then began to take ESP seriously.

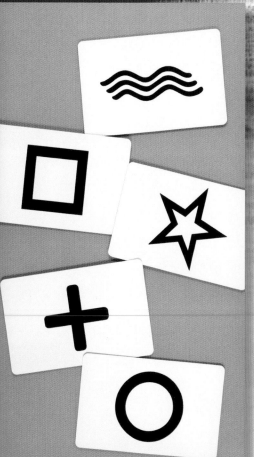

▼ **Zener cards were one of the first tools used to study ESP.**

EDGE FACT

▲ Dr. Rhine sat two volunteers far apart and then asked one volunteer to focus on a Zener card. The other volunteer wrote down the image that came to mind.

Chapter 3

Investigating a Sixth Sense

What triggers ESP? Can people learn to tap into their ESP abilities? Scientists hoped to answer these questions after they read about Dr. Rhine's studies.

Scientists explored ESP in different ways. Some thought that ESP abilities might be stronger when people are sleeping. They wanted to know if a relaxed brain was better able to receive ESP messages.

Learn about:
• ESP and dreams
• The ganzfeld method
• Remote viewing

Some people believe dreams can be part of ESP experiences.

In 1973, researchers Montague Ullman and Stanley Krippner published a book on dream research. During a 10-year period, the researchers used dream tests to study telepathy.

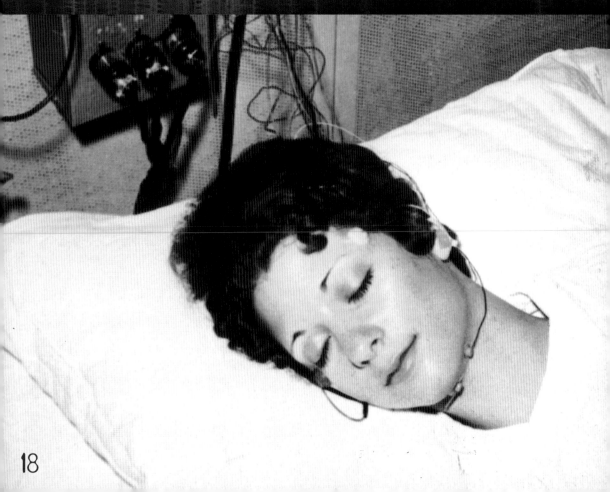

▼ In the 1970s, scientists studied dreams to learn about ESP.

Ullman and Krippner tried to use telepathy to influence a person's dreams. While a volunteer slept in a quiet room, a second volunteer in another room looked at a photograph. Scientists asked this volunteer to use telepathy to send a mental image of the photo to the sleeping person. The scientists then woke the sleeping person to find out if the person had any dreams. In studies with more than 100 volunteers, many people described images in their dreams that matched the photographs.

▼ Stanley Krippner used a machine to record volunteers' brain activity while they slept.

Blocking Out Senses

In the 1970s, scientist Charles Honorton began to research ESP. He wanted to know if ESP was stronger when other senses were blocked. He used a research method called the ganzfeld method.

During Honorton's experiments, a volunteer relaxed in a soundproof room. To block out light, Honorton covered the volunteer's eyes with padded Ping-Pong balls cut in half. In another room, a person tried to send the volunteer a selected image using telepathy.

Honorton was pleased with his ganzfeld tests. People with their vision and hearing blocked saw the correct image about 35 percent of the time.

Some skeptics say Honorton's tests didn't provide strong proof. But scientists around the world are still using the ganzfeld method to study ESP.

▲ ESP scientists use headphones and Ping-Pong balls to block out sound and sight. At the bottom are samples of images they might use for a ganzfeld experiment.

Government Gets Involved

From the 1970s to the early 1990s, leaders of the former Soviet Union studied ESP. They thought telepathy and clairvoyance would help agents uncover information about U.S. weapons and war plans.

U.S. government officials also began doing ESP research. They performed their research at SRI International in Menlo Park, California.

U.S. scientists Harold Puthoff and Russell Targ did many ESP experiments. They first asked volunteers to guess what was inside a locked box. Next, they moved on to harder experiments. They asked volunteers called senders to travel to the San Francisco Bay area. These volunteers then tried to send a mental image of what they saw back to a person at SRI. In many cases, the tests were successful.

EDGE FACT

In 1984, a woman in Russia described a merry-go-round that a California researcher was visiting 10,000 miles (16,000 kilometers) away.

▲ Some people with ESP can accurately describe a place even if they have never been there before.

ESP Visions of Outer Space

Later SRI experiments didn't use senders. Instead, volunteers were asked to imagine a faraway place and report what they saw there. Scientists called these studies remote viewing experiments.

In 1973, Puthoff and Targ asked volunteer Ingo Swann to do a remote viewing of the planet Jupiter. At that time, people knew little about the planet. But the scientists knew they would be able to prove or disprove Swann's information. NASA had scheduled a flight to study the planet.

During the experiment, Swann had a vision of a large planet with a ring around it. Photos later taken by NASA's spacecraft proved that Swann's vision was right. Jupiter does have faint rings around it. Swann also described Jupiter's color and atmosphere correctly.

⬆ Jupiter's orange color was one detail Ingo Swann saw in his remote viewing of the planet.

Chapter 4

Looking for Answers

Skeptics say ESP stories don't provide enough proof. Few people write down their predictions before an event. After an earthquake, people could claim they knew it was going to happen.

James Randi is a well-known ESP skeptic. He says scientists don't control their experiments closely enough. Randi says people can easily find out information in advance and then say it is ESP.

Learn about:
- Skeptics of ESP
- Computers in research
- Growing support for ESP

James Randi doesn't believe ESP evidence
is strong enough to prove it is real.

Search Continues

Recently, the evidence for ESP has become stronger. Scientists have run thousands of ganzfeld experiments. They used computers to produce random pictures and numbers that people tried to guess. Random pictures meant volunteers couldn't know the test answers ahead of time. Still, some people think the tests were fake. They believe people were told what the images would be before the tests began.

Although doubts still exist, scientists are finding it hard to ignore ESP research. In the future, someone may be able to prove beyond a doubt that humans really do have a sixth sense.

EDGE FACT

▲ Many people believe computers make ESP testing more accurate.

Glossary

clairvoyance (klair-VOY-uhns)—being able to sense people or events that are far away or unknown to most other people

extrasensory perception (EK-struh-SEN-sur-ee pur-SEP-shun)—the ability to sense something without using taste, touch, sight, smell, or hearing

precognition (pree-cog-NISH-uhn)—knowledge of a future event or situation

prediction (pri-DIKT-shuhn)—a person's statement of what they think will happen in the future

random (RAN-duhm)—without a specific order

remote viewing (ree-MOHT VYOO-ing)—envisioning a faraway place with one's mind

skeptic (SKEP-tic)—a person who questions things that other people believe in

telepathy (tuh-LEP-uh-thee)—communication between minds without use of the normal senses

Read More

Herbst, Judith. *ESP.* The Unexplained. Minneapolis: Lerner, 2005.

Netzley, Patricia D. *ESP.* Mystery Library. San Diego: Lucent Books, 2001.

Oxlade, Chris. *The Mystery of ESP.* Can Science Solve? Chicago: Heinemann, 2002.

Internet Sites

FactHound offers a safe, fun way to find Internet sites related to this book. All of the sites on FactHound have been researched by our staff.

Here's how:
1. Visit *www.facthound.com*
2. Type in this special code **0736854517** for age-appropriate sites. Or enter a search word related to this book for a more general search.
3. Click on the **Fetch It** button.

FactHound will fetch the best sites for you!

Index